Intoart: See The Revolutionary Art Exhibit

Whitechapel Gallery

7th November 2009 to 10th January 2010

For the year leading up to 'Intoart: See The Revolutionary Art Exhibit' and for a year after the exhibition, we recorded conversations, artists' talks, performances and workshops. Transcriptions of these recordings are presented here alongside writing by the artists. These conversations, developed over the last two years, accompany the artwork that made up the exhibition at the Whitechapel Gallery. This edited selection of statements, questions and answers echoes the system Ntiense Eno-Amooquaye establishes in her performance **See Revolutionary Art Exhibit**, which is also referenced in the title of our exhibition. We made this book to remember conversations that have taken place about the artworks (made in the Intoart studio) as they moved from our studio to the Whitechapel Gallery. This book is an opportunity to think together about questions that have arisen about this movement.
Questions about Intoart: What are the individual practices of the artists that make up Intoart and what does Intoart learn together as a collective that includes people with learning disabilities?
Questions about the artwork: What is lost or gained as artwork made in the Intoart studio is moved to the walls of the Whitechapel Gallery?
Questions about the exhibition: How does Intoart present what they do?

12th November 2009 – Exhibition opening at Whitechapel Gallery
Ntiense Eno-Amooquaye, Transcripton of See Revolutionary Art Exhibit *performance illustrated on pages 9 and 10*

The statement

The artwork atmosphere of culture means to recommend and recognize the example of same and different life and future and to see the art of the exhibit. To integrate words to see revolutionary atmosphere of culture on the version. To supervise is to recall improvisation words.

To Ask Questions

1. What do you know about the exhibit ?

The art exhibit is about to make the words improvise, to comprehend the word exhibit. To move the words into the Whitechapel to make immigration of words.

All Of The Questions

1. How do you supervise the words?

The supervisation of words means ways of contributing and contrasting the words meaning the same and different. The solution to make sure that the words are like the solving like having problems and making clear and clean to provide the correct words and the meaning of words.

2. Where do you get the improvisation words from and what do the words mean?
The word improvisation is from the words and imagination to regulate and recognize, to talk and to hear, to listen well. Improvise is to give more words and to present new words and old words and to create words.

<u>The new words</u>
Improceve
Verovisation
Wonder wellewheel
Conternete
Prepeent
Proseve

28th November 2009 - Panel discussion at Whitechapel Gallery
Sam Jones, Introduction
As I watched Ntiense perform at the opening of the exhibition, I was transported back to the Intoart studio where she started to write **See Revolutionary Art Exhibit**; projecting the words onto the studio wall, using her system of statement, question and answer to develop her own account of seeing the Revolutionary Art Exhibit. Her performance lasted 20 minutes and required people to read each word, as she wrote, her words projected onto a large screen. As Ntiense performed in the creative studio (a long, broad space at the top of the Whitechapel Gallery) time seemed to slow down. There was silence and although the space was full, Ntiense held the audiences' attention and set the pace by which we read her words. So what changed as Ntiense performed this piece at the Whitechapel Gallery in front of an audience?

When I first read the following extract from Tony Parkers' oral biography of Studs Terkel (oral historian and broadcaster) it brought Ntiense's invitation to **See Revolutionary Art Exhibit** immediately to mind.

> There was this black woman one time, I saw her standing in the street, with two or three of her kids round her and she was looking at - and you know what? There's nothing in the window. She's looking in an empty shop window – looking at nothing. So naturally I'm curious – naturally I'm curious – So I say "Excuse me ma'am – but what are you looking at?" She doesn't seem to mind being spoken to by a stranger, and she doesn't turn her head around to see who's asking her or anything, and after a moment or so she says "Oh" she says "Oh, dreams, I'm just looking at dreams." So I've got my tape recorder and I switch it on and I say "Good dreams, bad dreams...?" And she starts to talk. Then she talks a little bit more, and a little bit more. And her kids are playing around her, and they can see I'm tape recording what their Mom is saying, and when she stops talking after eight maybe ten minutes or so one of them says, "Heh Mom, can we listen to what you said?" And I ask her if it's ok with her and she says yes, so I play it back and she listens to it too. And when it's over, she gives a little shake of her head and she looks at me, and she says "well until I heard that, I never knew I felt that way." [1]

The audience in this account changes as the 'dreams' change from unspoken to spoken, from unseen to seen. An audience exists in the Intoart studio that changes in a similar way. We are an audience acting collectively to see and hear one and other, changing over time as people make new work in the studio and see that work performed, screened, exhibited or published in a book. Ntiense ends her performance by writing a list of invented new words. I asked Ntiense as she was writing in the studio to explain what the new word, 'wonder wellewheel' means. She answered, 'The wonder wellewheel is if you desire and inspire to think and talk.' Ntiense's performance connects us to her own experience of the studio, inviting us to 'desire and inspire to think and talk.'

1. Studs Terkel: A Life in Words
Tony Parker - HarperCollins - 1997

28th November 2009 – Panel Discussion at Whitechapel Gallery
Ella Ritchie, Rob Tufnell, Harold Offeh and Sam Jones

Ella: Both yourself and Rob have visited the studio and there are conversations that I suppose precede the hanging of the work, particularly here at the Whitechapel Gallery. And I wonder if you experience any loss, whether we gain anything from the work coming from the studio to the gallery, do you think we lose or gain anything and what are those things?

Rob: I think yes, probably you do slightly but I think you gain other things. One of the things that I found really kind of impressive about the Intoart studio is that people are doing their thing day to day, and obviously my being there made it different, but all the individuals involved all had a very different activity and they all come from very different backgrounds. There's this great atmosphere and there's a lot of humour, but there's a lot of seriousness as well and it seems to be a very functional studio in that way. There doesn't appear to be a lot of egos, big egos competing with one and other. Transferring it to the gallery I think some of the humour is lost, although I think the film Lenka Clayton made with Ntiense Eno-Amooquaye is excellent for that because I think that brings some of it back in.

Ella: The reasons we approached those films was exactly that, to try and bring some of the studio into the gallery but then we tread that careful line of it not being documentation of a process, but actually standing up in its own right as an artwork. Are people (coming to see the exhibition) responding to individual artists or are people responding to the collective? Harold you visited the studio, in terms of meeting people together, what do you think of the notion of the collective versus the individual?

Harold: It's quite interesting how that's reconciled. There's a classic art collective model of individuals being subsumed within this brand identity – maybe that's a rather crude way of putting it. What interested me in your structure is that Intoart becomes a kind of platform for the individuals, and there's a kind of constituent sense of very specific individual identities. And Intoart is a kind of framework that allows for discussion and dialogue to happen in-between these individuals. From the experience of going to the studio (you can see it in the website as well) it's very clear, that these are very separate artists with differing concerns. But there is also something about this collective conversation that's being generated that feeds those individual practices. And the interest lies in-between this dualism of the collective and the individuals.

Sam: I think our point is to argue about things sometimes – we do argue about things – and I think that's important. That is something that means that we can be (rather than a model) a practice that grows with time, that has a story, that has a history and responds to new experiences.

Rob: I think the thing about Intoart is that it isn't about pre-conceived outcomes and it isn't about trying to control people. It's about trying to give people a platform and an opportunity and an environment where they can work collectively and do what they need to do and this is Intoart's success and its failure as a collective something I am still trying to get my head around.

04th December 2009 – Whitechapel Gallery
Ella Ritchie, Malcolm Bull and members of Intoart talking about the exhibition.

Whitechapel Gallery invited writer and art historian Malcolm Bull to write a new text for the exhibition. His text uses words spoken or written by the artists in the Intoart studio. The text was pasted onto the wall of the gallery in two columns. In response to the following exchange between Malcolm and Ella while the exhibition was still up at the Whitechapel Gallery, we re-photographed the text on the wall of our studio (pages 7 and 8).

Ella: Before the exhibition we spoke about reading out your text and the potential, not necessarily of performing it, but of just reading it out loud. We read the text today in the studio now that the exhibition is up and it really made sense in the studio. Are you interested in the difference between the words being written and being said?

Malcolm: Most of the things in the text were originally said, some of them were written, but most of them were probably originally said and said in the studio, so reading it out in the studio is taking it back to its original context from which its been extracted and maybe the words seem like they've come back home in a sense.

I came into the art project

Intoart is an organisation that is to do with nothing but art

the artwork is like a theme of work

when you do a theme... it's in a line... when you have all this work that is there in a line it's like a theme

line shapes the shape of it looks like a map

shapes are like a jungle or a maze like the branches of a tree like different entries and booby traps

the escape is... to run or go in the hole to break the wall... to escape from the wall to wall and have a hole in the wall

the open door wider of cave that opens has dark shadow

first we hear the sound of saying hello

then we hear the sound of screaming

this lady has her hand over her mouth

she feels awe and shocked

her eyes in her eyeball is white

when I see my face in the mirror I see a lot shading

the light and dark shadings look like there is a real person

someone has got to hold and help her to walk slow

when I start work... the different marks have to be gentle

I just take my time

I pay attention to all details

I can't see the left ear because the hair is long and dark

I like to work hard with my artwork

glad that I ask if every detail is all right

posh woman

the hair is tied all the way down to the back

roman woman

I do the hair all wavy in the right style

vacant look

he has a very bad hair day... he asked for a trim but got a bit of a shock

self-portrait

the thing is with the hair that you have to cover it with a head tie... a head scarf. That's how to do your hair it goes on your head

when I got used to using the pastels... I did it because it was nice and messy

my fingers feel dry because I am shading in willow charcoal

why did you choose these materials?

he said that the material was from Ghana and I said yes

by photocopying the art picture from the artbook

because the paper looks quite rough

because I like to draw and colour

why did you choose these materials?

to have words on artwork and know about art

stones are the subject of my work

at first he was a human being then he got bitten by a vampire
how do you supervise the words?
to supervise is to recall
memories of people that have died
being in touch with people and having photos
what do you love about rocks?
There are loads of them and you can pick any one you want to take
I feel the texture
I don't do it from memory
that person is in black coming towards her
she feels that she has forgotten something
the colour suits Dracula

some of the colours come forward and some of them go back
her teeth are blue and white
the cave is made with hard stone and brown soil
when I mix colours on a palette the colour starts to change.
The colour changes as many times as I want it to change
words integrate to explain how you want to
I am interested in mixing shapes to make a new shape that
people haven't seen before
do you ever see the words integrate?
I start drawing the different shapes by making one shape then
I overlap the shapes
improceve, verovisation, wonder wellewheel, conternete, prepeent, proseve
the wonder wellewheel is if you desire and inspire

we like to have a laugh
the atmosphere in the studio is very good
why do you think that is?
it is about an atmosphere of culture
like David Hockney's drawings
when I am drawing I am thinking about... to have a holiday abroad and
visit some galleries in another country
might go back to Ghana next year
me and Ella went to Brighton
I go to church and we meet there
I would like people to feel quiet when they look at my work
to have education is to improve the experience of the arts

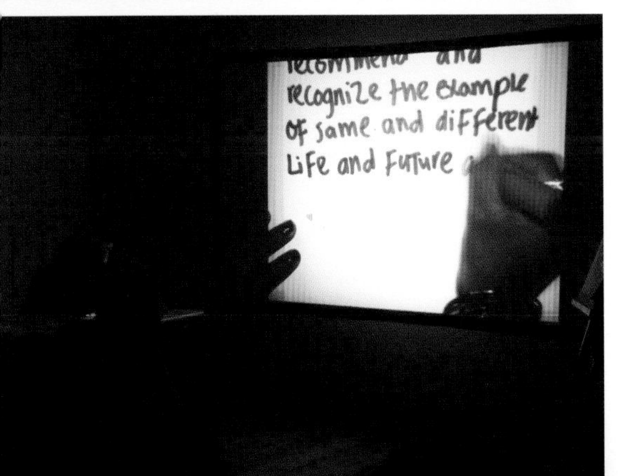

See Revolutionary Art Exhibit
Performed at Whitechapel Gallery, 2009
Ntiense Eno-Amooquaye

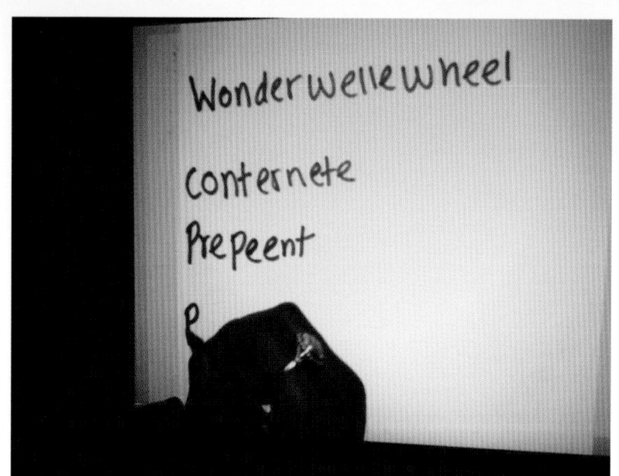
Wonderwellewheel
conternete
Prepeent

THE Statement
The art work atmosphere
of culture

SOMEONE HAS GOT TO
HOLD AND HELP HER TO
WALK SLOW AND NEED
TO HELP HER WALK.

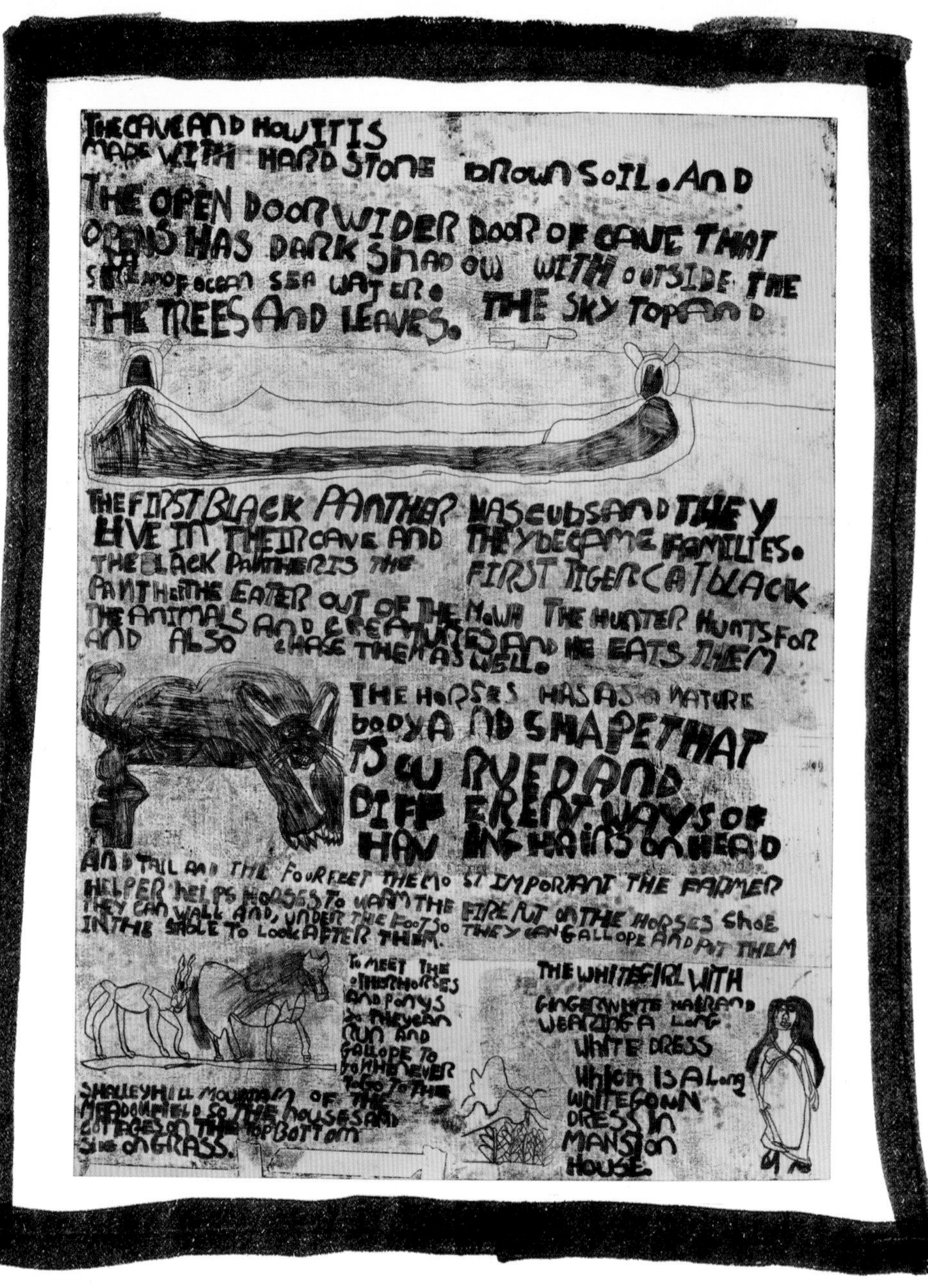

THE art exhibit is about to make the words improvise to comprehend THE word exhibit. To move the words into the White Chapel to make immigration OF words.

Page 11
Under the Sea
Chalk pastel and ink on paper
35cm x 40cm

Someone has got to Hold her
Monoprint
42cm x 60cm

Page 12 (top)
The Cave Echoes
Monoprint
112cm x 84cm

Ntiense Eno-Amooquaye

Harry Potters dad

2

The history of this particular portrait that I have drawn on paper he has got a confused expression on his face because I like to deal with art but with portraits in particular with expressions on a portraits face.
Because with portraits they are just like me apart from the portrait being drawn onto a piece of paper.
I am a real person with emotions and feelings and instincts e.g. because I am the artist drawing the portrait and not the other way around.

Page 14
Issues
Chalk pastel on paper
77cm x 56cm

Page 15
Harry Potter's Dad
Charcoal on paper
44cm x 38cm

This page
Mr and Mrs
Chalk pastel on paper
77cm x 56cm

Clifton Wright

1. **Issues** 2. **Mr and Mrs** 3. **Mr Potato Head** 4. **Egg Head** 5. **Twisted Man's Face** 6. **Chalked Man** 7. **Upper Class Boy** 8. **The Wedding Couple** 9. **Man in a White Suit** 10. **Marilyn Monroe** 11. **School Boy** 12. **Portrait of a Faded Man** 13. **Posh Woman**

8th April 2010 - Intoart studio

Rob Tufnell and Clifton Wright looking at Clifton's studio wall

Rob: What attracted you to the idea of making drawings, was it some sense that this was something you wanted to do, that you liked the idea of it?

Clifton: I liked the idea of it because it gave me a way to express myself, and it just works. It works. I am confident in drawing, yeah it's just making it realistic of how it looks, like with the expression.

R: Were there particular artists that inspired you, for example behind you've got a David Hockney book and Tal R book and both of them are brilliant artists but one makes what might be traditionally understood as representational drawing and paintings, whilst Tal R does his own thing and has his own vocabulary. Was there a particular artist that gave you confidence or particularly inspired you in what you do?

C: I don't think there was, it gave me confidence but there was no artist. I looked at the books, that's how I got the inspiration and I just drawed all the portraits that I done, really realistic, really good I mean.
R: Because I think you've got your own vocabulary, and there are things in the pictures that remind me of other artists but I never get the sense that your looking at them and making your own work, you've really developed your own visual language.
C: Yeah
R: Have you always used colour or is this something you're starting to introduce more recently?
C: When I started Intoart, I wasn't really doing much colour or drawing, I was doing mostly sculptures and it was just the space we had [Animal, Mineral, Vegetable project at South London Gallery]. I forgot what I was going to say, sugar.
R: And how did you feel about doing that, was it something that you enjoyed doing but didn't do what you needed it to do, or...
C: I enjoyed what I was doing but I knew there was something else with Intoart I could do, portraits and shapes.
R: And the abstract works you were doing with shapes do you see these portraits linking with those or do you see them as completely separate?
C: I say both because some portraits I can use for using shapes to draw people.
R: Thinking of what I have seen of your work before, people might think that these drawings are done very quickly but how long does it take you to do a drawing like that?
C: Well when it's actually finished, it's about two or three weeks; sometimes two, three or four weeks.
R: Because I think that's quite important because they look like you might have really rushed them and when I have seen you working it's an incredibly methodical and thought out process where you really consider things.
C: Yeah
R: Have you worked with paint ever?
C: I've used water based and acrylic paint as well. I tried it, but it didn't really... I liked it for a while but I just wanted to do something else like use different materials.
R: And how do you think you go from here, do you think you are going to change your subject matter at all or your materials? Or do you think you've found your thing now?

Clockwise from left

Marilyn Monroe
Graphite and oil pastel on paper
30cm x 21cm

Portrait of a Faded Man
Charcoal and oil pastel on paper
30cm x 21cm

School Boy
Charcoal on paper
46cm x 60cm

Clifton Wright

C: I found my thing, what I like doing.
R: Do you see your work improving, or do you see it as pretty much consistent?
C: Pretty much consistent.
R: Which is your favourite on this wall?
C: There aint no favourites.
R: They're not your favourites?
C: No, they're all my favourites, I've got no favouritism.
R: Do you ever abandon a picture; you're half way through and then you give up on it?
C: If I'm not too happy drawing the head I just try again, I don't give up.
R: So you keep working on it until it works?
C: Yeah
R: And that's why it often takes a long time?
C: Yeah
R: How often do you come into the studio?
C: Every –well when we had the funding– it was about every Friday.
R: And do you work at home, or at other times?
C: No I don't, but I go and have a look at other exhibitions by myself.
R: But do you do drawings in your notebook?
C: No I don't, I just do notes and that's it.
R: And what sort of notes do you write, ideas for drawings?
C: No it's the other way around 'cause whatever I've drawn and coloured in and finished, I just write it down [give the work titles and write about the portrait].
R: And what else do you do, what else informs the way you make work? You go and look at exhibitions and do you read books, do you watch TV, films, I mean I know this comes from a Batman film but I don't remember which one it is?
C: Dark Knight
R: Do films inspire you?
C: Films do inspire me, just depends what type of taste it is.
R: But this drawing on the top left the **Posh Woman** is that from a photograph or is it someone you actually saw?
C: I think it was from a book in here but I don't know which one it was.
R: It looks a little bit to me like Frida Kahlo.
C: I don't know who that is to be honest.
R: The picture underneath says Diego Rivera and he was her husband but that's just coincidence.

C: Ok
R: These pencil drawings I've not seen these before, are these new things your doing?
C: They are just little experiments.
R: So are they sketches for the works that are charcoal and oil pastel?
C: Some are and some, mainly some of them are yeah.
R: And this one here next to **Harry Potter's Dad** can you tell me about that one?
C: That was from a book and, oh I'm trying to remember it, 'cause the head was at a different angle and I gave myself a little bit of a tricky task because all these heads apart from that one are straight. So I wanted to draw it at a different angle.
R: Was this a challenge for you because her face is slightly to the side and the same with **Twisted Man's Face**. Their faces are turned to the side rather than facing you directly?
C: It was a bit of a challenge that, yeah.
R: Do you think your work is confrontational, do you think it challenges people? I mean for example, if you really stare at someone like this it's quite intimidating and in a lot of your work these faces are not always very happy, they're not friendly faces.
C: No
R: They're in a way quite confrontational, is that deliberate that your trying to confront people?
C: No, because even though none of these portraits are smiling they are not meant to be confrontational or intimidating, there is an ok mood.
R: So are you pacifying them in a way, because I mean this character is in jail, what's he called?
C: What the film or character?
R: No, the picture.
C: The title is **Issues**.
R: **Issues**, so he's got issues and those are presented, I think you talked about it before. He's in jail isn't he?
C: Yeah
R: And the bars are sort of reflected in his face, and in these other areas.
C: Yep
R: I mean, I don't think they are confrontational, they could be, but they're not. Is it deliberate that they're not?
C: Even though they look confrontational I was trying to make sure they weren't.

R: They weren't. That's what I meant. So you're trying in a way to pacify them, maybe? But the other thing is you talk about them always as portraits but are they really portraits? Or is portraiture the vehicle by which you experiment with colour and light and dark and form and all these abstract ideas?
C: Yeah they are because portraits can be whatever you want it to be.
R: But this I think is a drawing of David Hockney [**Harry Potter's Dad**], but it's not a portrait of David Hockney.
C: No
R: But is it a portrait of Harry Potter's Dad, or is it a self-portrait? Is it a portrait of yourself or is it a portrait of just a generic person?
C: I don't know. I think the reason I gave it the title **Harry Potter's Dad** is because it looks like him because of the glasses that's in front of his eyes.
R: Does Harry Potter have a dad or are you imagining what Harry Potter's dad would look like if he had one?
C: Yeah
R: Cause I think that's part of the point of the book is that he doesn't have a dad, isn't it?
C: I think he did but I don't know?
R: Well he must have done.
C: Yeah
(Both laugh)
R: I think the whole thing is he's bought up by these people, his Uncle and Aunt or something, who he doesn't like.
C: Yeah
R: And then he goes off to this Hogwarts place.
C: Yeah
R: So it's almost like by doing a drawing of **Harry Potter's Dad** your drawing something that doesn't really exist.
C: Yeah
R: So that's what I mean about them not being really portraits, instead they are portraits from your own imagination, they're not portraits of specific people.
C: I know what you mean now.
R: So in a way I think they become like self-portraits because they're from your head not from you looking at someone and trying to express who they are.
C: Yeah true.

28th November 2009 – Panel discussion at Whitechapel Gallery

Ella Ritchie and Harold Offeh

Ella: The two gallery spaces we are exhibiting in are quite particular within this institution, in that they are programmed by the education department, although they give weight to the work by being very visible and not being in an education space. So I suppose it would be good to really explore in terms of artists (who do work and take seriously art education and art practice, which we do) is what are the limitations? Harold you're an artist working in both those fields, what are the limitations both curatorially or in the gallery department you might find yourself in?

Harold: It's often the kind of parameter you work with. There is an issue of institutional hierarchy, if you look at the institutional structure in terms of the curatorial department, the education, learning department – there is a hierarchy. They are both frameworks for the institution working with artists. But often the key thing (and we've discussed this before) is the dissemination and presentation of those kinds of encounters and the invitations and commissions that are set up by that. Obviously within a learning/education department there's a sense in which there is this kind of clearly marked benefit in terms of the participants and there is a structural coming together of these other people that your going to work with in terms of that. So the institution is foregrounding the parameters you're working with, as an artist you come in and respond to that. Where as in a curatorial department it tends to be the other way around, the institution is responding to your own given agenda. I find both ways really interesting in terms of working but for me I think Rob's touched on it in terms of how that then becomes disseminated, traditionally in learning departments. Because it's about the relationship between the artist and the participants or the community group, and that is what's seen as the most important thing. What comes out of that doesn't necessarily go beyond that, and often it's seen as problematic how that work is displayed and presented. And for me that's always the difficulty because then it becomes slightly marginalised within your practice, because it isn't subjected to the same sort of discourse, that other areas of your practice are.

Ella: When we were talking earlier, we were talking about the making of individual artworks being potentially more problematic than the notion of a performance or the screening of a film. Dealing with artworks and bringing those to the gallery and taking that seriously as well as those overarching benefits. We whole-heartedly acknowledge those benefits as being really important to what we do, but don't always make them visible in exhibitions.

Written responses by people taking part in the writing workshop that accompanied the exhibition at Whitechapel Gallery led by Ntiense Eno-Amooquaye and Sam Jones. People taking part in the workshop responded to the exhibition and to questions Ntiense Eno-Amooquaye asks in her text **See Revolutionary Art Exhibit**

Exhibition at Whitechapel Gallery

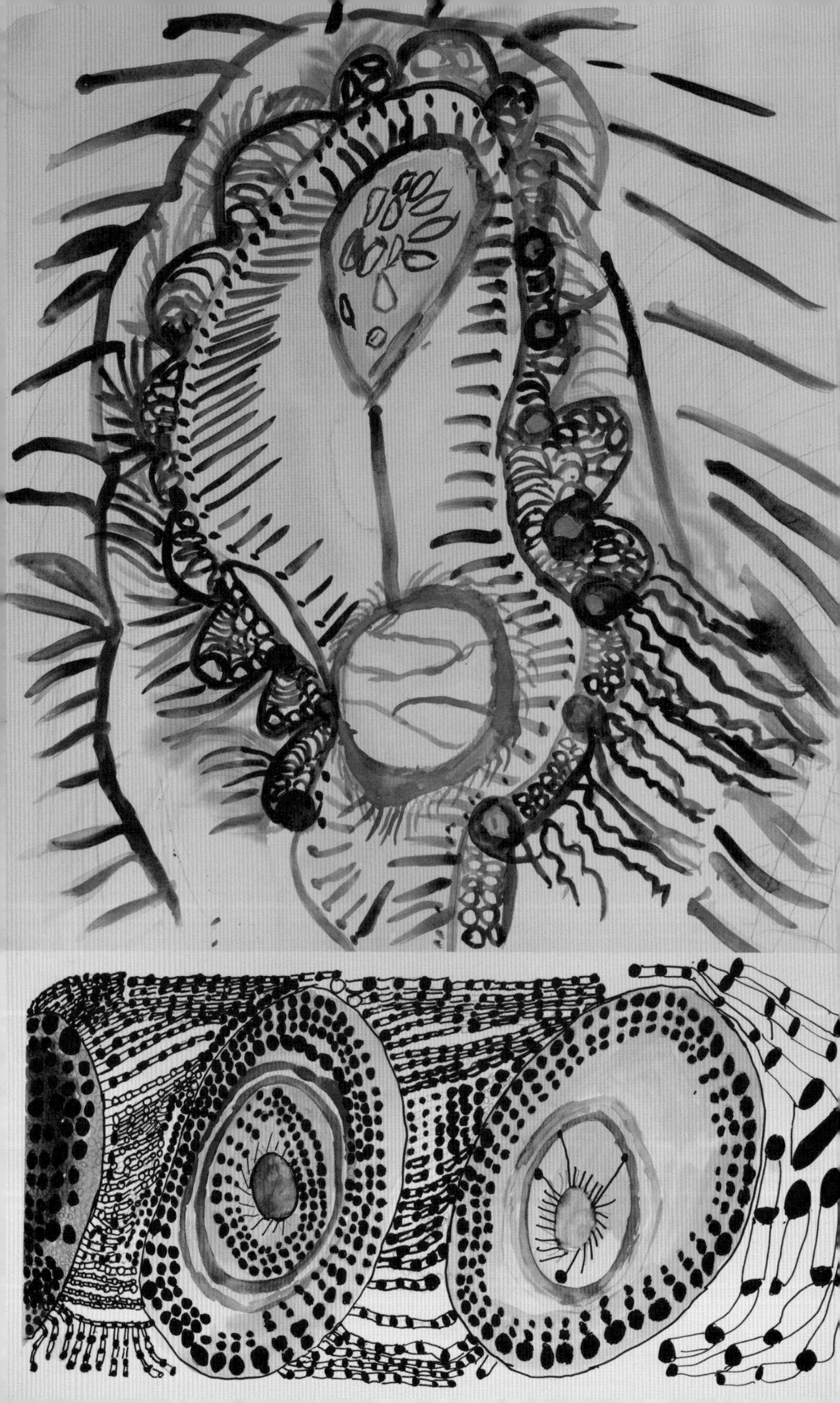

(1) HAVE you Been to Ghana (2) yes MANY times
(3) DiD you take these Photographs (4) That's my Aunty
(5) AND that's me Inside the tAXi (6) yes that's my
mum, that's my Aunty and that's my Aunty again and
My BiG BrotheR (7) So did you Like the orchard
(8) yes that's just me that's my mum that's my
Aunty......and that's me (9) .....and that's me with
my Boy (10) wow VERY handsome.......So would
Like to live in Ghana (11) yes 12 would you miss London
(13) yes 14 what do you like? DO you like the food
(15) yes might Go Back to Ghana next year. (16) Are
you going over there? with your mum?
(17) yes My Mum and my Aunty and My Big Brother
18 so why are they dressed in the same way?
19 Because this they always wear different
20 outfits. Because they have different tops
I have the old one at home. 21 They are all
from the Same family? 22 yes, I Like that. 23 I
love the dress its Beautiful 24 That's my mother
with some of the nurses and doctors 25 what is
She doing? Does she work at a hospital 26 yes
27 So when you look at Photograph's maureen what
are you looking at? What are you looking for?
28 PeopLe 29 and what else? what else do you
look for 30 Different Kind of fabrics and happy
faces Of the people 31 that's me 32 where's this
33 it's a church 34 I go twice a day at 10am and in

the evening at 6.30 35 ARe you going to Ghana
this summer? 36 yes but I haven't got the
ticket yet. 37 that's my uncles there 38 what
was the celebration there 39 when we go to
church and dance 40 There he is sitting on the
Road and then that's me standing besides him
41 so now you are painting patterns instead of
People? 42 yes 43 ARe you going to mix Both 44
I Look at the memory of it ... memories of
People that have died . memories
45 That's someone's mum . And that's me
outside in my Nightie . 46 So what do they ask
you to Bring when you visit them? 47 Photos
(laughs) 48 Is there a special food that you eat
a funeral? 49 yes ocre soup mmm... (laughs)
50 That's my mum 51 That's her in home,
that's the outside and then ... 52 That one?
53 That's a long time ago

This page
Perfect
Acrylic on canvas
76cm x 72cm

Page 30
From Ghana
Acrylic on canvas
86cm x 76cm

Page 31
Self Portrait
Charcoal on paper
62cm x 45cm

Mawuena Kattah

CRabs tortoise Binds SNake

rocodile

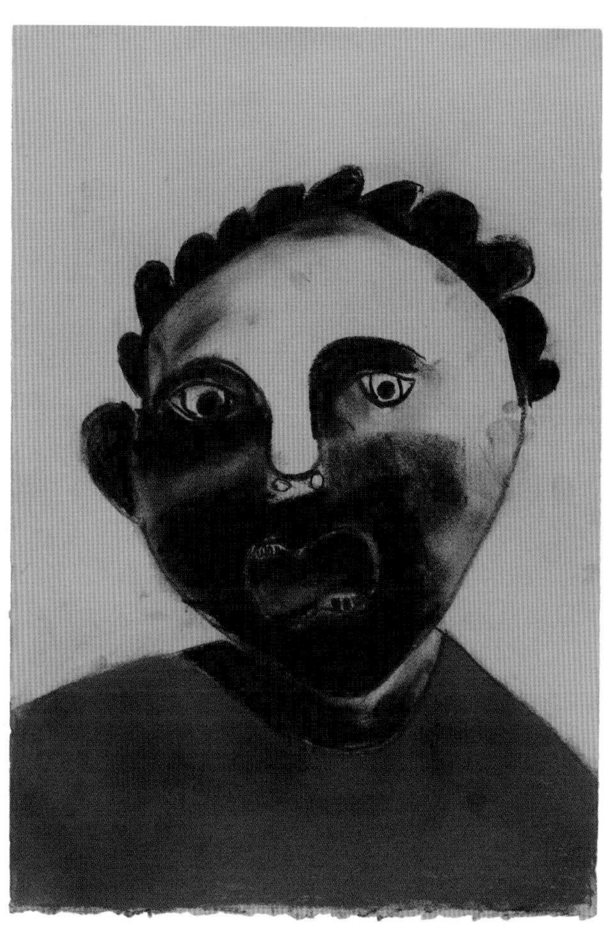

11th March 2010 – Intoart Studio
Ashley Whitfield, Mawuena Kattah, Ntiense Eno-Amooquaye and Clifton Wright

Ashley: While looking at your family photos from Ghana (Mawuena) I wondered if you could describe the difference between a family and a collective? Is there a difference? Would you describe Intoart as a family?
Mawuena: All my family come from Ghana, and sometimes I go visit Accra, Ho, Tema, all that. I like to paint pictures of my family, taking photos from Ghana, then get the film developed then I do it on paper at Intoart. I talk about the Intoart studio at Studio Voltaire to my family, talk about doing different pictures, watercolour pictures and taking photos from Ghana.
A: I noticed in your films at Whitechapel that you often seem to work alone. In each of your films it was just you, doing your own work or instructing the camera. I wondered if you could describe the importance of working on your own versus working within a group?
Ntiense: It's like in a team you have to discuss over, things like ideas, do the planning for that as well. The team is like when you talk and take notes, that's how you have your plan for in the future and ideas for it as well.
A: Does everyone have a chance to make decisions in your collective?
Clifton: Yes, we do have an opinion but we ask for advice at the same time. I'm used to working by myself always on that table but if I have to change then I don't mind but at the same time I'm not too bothered about people being in the Intoart studio as long as they are doing what needs to be done, that's it.
A: Do you think that Intoart would work if each person came on a different day, by themselves, or is it important that there are meeting times for artists to come together?
C: There needs to be meeting times because of people knowing what needs to be done, or what they want to do next in the future.
A: Do you think it's important for your work to communicate with other artist's work in your collective?
C: With my portraits, how I first started off with face portraits, Ella said to me, 'What do I want to do for the future?' last year and asked me would I like to do portraits because I'd done a self portrait of myself two years ago and it really went well and I did all those face portraits and I decided for myself, nobody told me what to do, I decided for myself to do the whole body portrait, I did quite a lot of them actually. What about you, do you prefer to work on your own or with people?
A: Sometimes it's good to be able to say ideas out loud to someone.
C: I do that too.

11th December 2009 – Whitechapel Gallery

Selina Helene speaks to Ntiense Eno-Amooquaye about her paintings while Ntiense writes down her words

First One
Did the drawing first, choose the colour you want then paint it, then the same draw the picture choose the colour then paint, draw the picture to choose, I colour what I want then paint it.

Second One
Then the same to draw picture what I want then I choose the colour then paint
Green
Blue
Purple
Bit of red

Third One
You draw then choose colour and paint in what
Colour
Pink
Brown
Blue
Red
I draw the shapes then choose the
Paints
Red
Blue
Green

Fourth One
I draw the shapes
Then choose the water
Paint then paint in the different shapes

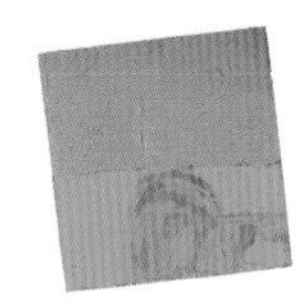
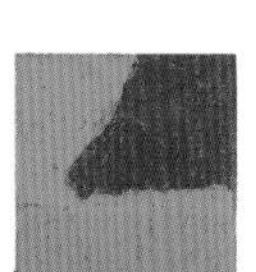
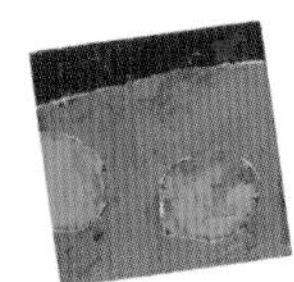

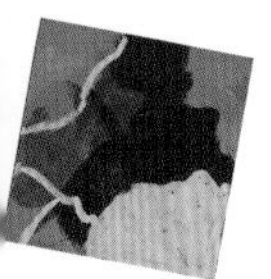

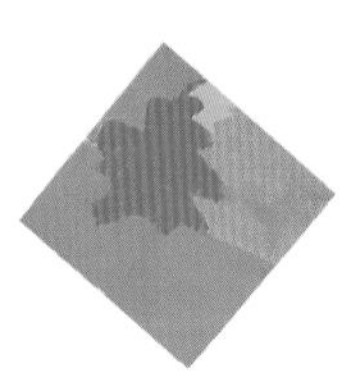

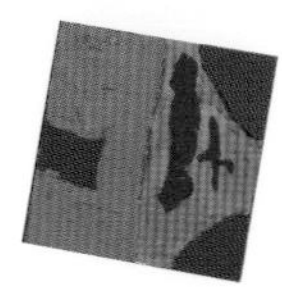
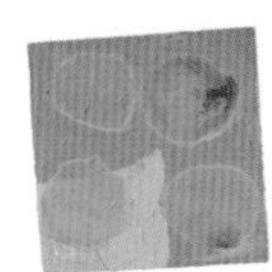

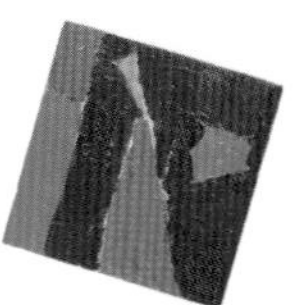
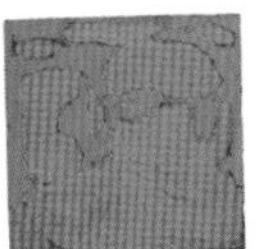

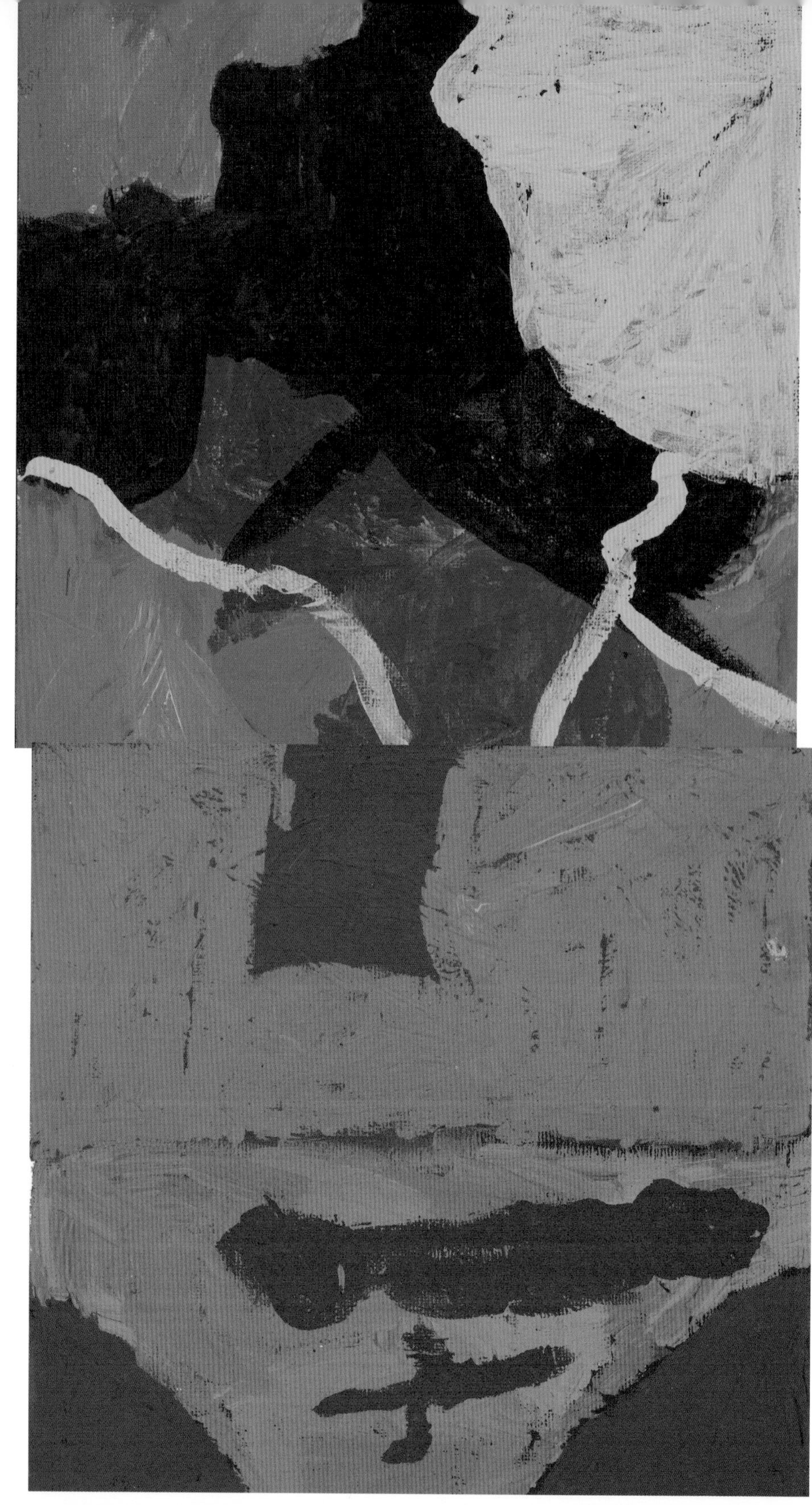

Pages 34, 35, 36
Different Shapes
Acrylic on canvas
20cm x 20cm

Selina Helene

19th April 2010

Hello Philomena,
I have been looking at two of your pictures **Water Flower** and **Firework Flower** with Clifton in your studio at Studio Voltaire. I enjoyed doing this very much. Thank you for asking me questions about your work. I think the flowers in your painting **Water Flower** look wilder and looser, the colours are very rich which is strange as a lot of the colours have been washed out or have been made using lots of water. There is a balance between the red and the greens and I love the top left hand side with the very pale blue marks, there but almost not there.
Here are a few questions from me to you.
1. Which of the two pictures is your favourite and why?
2. Would you ever make a really small painting of flowers?
3. This might seem a bit of a strange question but I like to ask it of artists. When did you decide to be an artist?

P.S. There is a wonderful French artist called Pierre Bonnard who painted beautiful pictures in oil and watercolour of tables with flowers and food on them. Tate Britain has several of his works. He was very fond of Dachshunds and had one as a pet.

With Best Wishes
Daniel

24th June 2010

Hello Daniel,
Thank you for looking at my pictures, the **Firework Flower** is my favourite. I like the colours and how I drawed them. It looks like the fireworks. It's a different style, the other one is quite flat. In the **Firework Flower** I like the background. I like how I did all the patterns at the back, it looks like a forest. I like all of it. Yes, it would be a different thing to do a small painting and it might take a while. I'd have to draw it and colour it. There would be more details to it. I didn't decide to be an artist, I like doing the artwork because its calmful and I like doing it. It's different when we work longer and decide what we want to do.

Thanks
Philomena

Page 39
Water Flower
Pen on paper
38cm x 51cm

Opposite page
Firework Flower
Pen on paper
52cm x 36cm

Philomena Powell

The lady has her hand over her mouth.

She looks all that scared.

That person is in black coming towards her and all that makes the place all dark.

She feels that she has forgotten something.

She is in thought.

She feels all

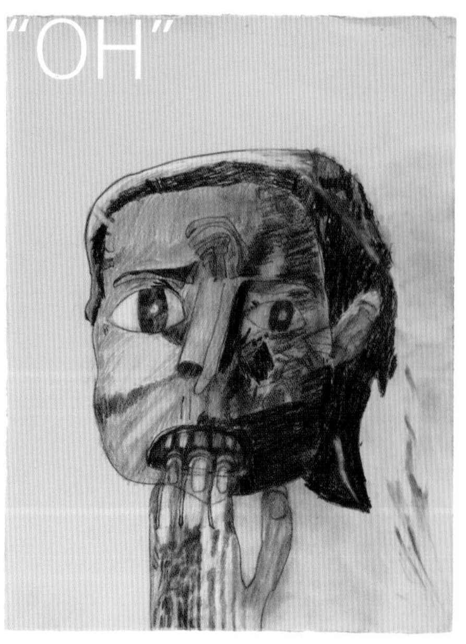

and shook up herself. Just then she feels all in shock.

Her hand is fingers and thumbs, her thumb is a bit bendy and her hand is

Page 42
Lady with Hand over her Mouth
Graphite and pencil on paper
56cm x 42cm

Page 43
Two Heads
Graphite and pencil on paper
92cm x 122cm

Opposite page
Man in Dark Room
Graphite and pencil on paper
84cm x 60cm

This page left to right:
Lady with Straight Long Hair
Lady with Plaited Hair in a Bun
Lady Wearing Cane Roll to her Shoulders
Graphite and pencil on paper
63cm x 48cm

Doreen McPherson

[illegible]

Individual Practice and Collective Action

This exhibition challenged us to present what we do at the Whitechapel Gallery, a gallery presenting an international programme of contemporary and 20th century art in the heart of East London. By putting our work in Whitechapel's gallery spaces, next to the British Council collection and alongside exhibitions of internationally established artists, a large number of people visiting the gallery encountered Intoart for the first time. This visibility of an inclusive practice where people with and without learning disabilities share a creative exchange presented new challenges for the gallery and audiences.

Our story so far has been enriched by our activity in the fields of art, education and learning disability. Ntiense Eno-Amooquaye writes in the studio 'to have education is to improve the experience of the arts.' Clifton Wright disagrees with this sentence in relation to his own experience of the studio and making art. He says, 'Art has helped me to improve my education.' He reflects on this further in the film he made with Lenka Clayton, 'Drawing helps you do something with your life. That you have the skills and knowledge of what you are good at. Plus it gives you something to achieve. And it makes you experiment with where you want to go.' These different experiences of education evoke moments of change, resisting a definition where 'one size fits all' in favour of an openness to listen to each other and find ways for peoples' voices to be heard.

In the studio, where artwork is made and reciprocal learning takes place, questions of authorship and democracy remain important to the integrity of our activity and how we present what we do. Looking outward from the studio, our activities in galleries inquisitively negotiate their education and curatorial departments. These activities both raise questions about how we talk to curators about what we do and an awareness that the gallery's use of language can take hold of the articulation and positioning of our work. The time spent in the gallery and making this book demanded a closer interrogation of our work through dialogue and debate, outside of the collective. In the studio, people have the opportunity to find a relationship to writing and talking about themselves, their ideas and experiences. Here, limitations and narrow interpretations of literacy and academic achievement are challenged by bringing to the fore some witty, experimental, insightful and sometimes poignant articulations of what it means to make art.

Sam Jones and Ella Ritchie

Intoart: See The Revolutionary Art Exhibit
7th November 2009 - 10th January 2010
Public events
Artist Talks and Performances 12th November 2009
Workshop Day 20th November 2009
Panel Discussion 28th November 2009

Published by Intoart
c/o 38 Albert Road, Leyton, London E10 6NX
Email info@intoart.org.uk
www.intoart.org.uk

Co-edited and produced by
Sam Jones and Ella Ritchie
Design and typesetting by
Andrew Bannister and the artists
www.andrew-bannister.com
Artwork photographed by Marcus Leith
Proofread by Ashley Whitfield

Front cover image **Lady with Plaited Hair in a Bun**
by Doreen McPherson

Intoart would like to thank
Artdata, Andrew Preston (Director, Rathbone), Joe Scotland (Artistic Director, Studio Voltaire), Whitechapel Gallery, the contributors to the book and those who took part in our workshops and events.

Printed by Calverts www.calverts.coop
ISBN 9780948835445

INTOART

Intoart Projects is a registered charity 1106084
Company Limited by Guarantee (England) No 5215861

Whitechapel Gallery

Films by Lenka Clayton with Ntiense Eno-Amooquaye, Mawuena Kattah, Doreen McPherson and Clifton Wright.

The films are made from four different points of view and tell stories about the studio and about the artists whose work they explore. They were shown as part of the exhibition.